THE HISTORY DETECTIVE INVESTIGATES

EVACUATION IN WORLD WAR II

Martin Parsons

D0230987

This paperback edition published in 2015

Copyright © Wayland 2015

Dewey Number: 940.5'3161'0941
ISBN: 978 0 7502 9639 7

10 9 8 7 6 5 4 3 2 1

MIX
Paper from
responsible sources
FSC® C104740

Editor: Jason Hook
Designer: Simon Borrough
Cartoon artwork: Richard Hook

Wayland, an imprint of
Hachette Children's Group
Part of Hodder & Stoughton
Carmelite House
50 Victoria Embankment
London EC4Y 0DZ

Printed in China

An Hachette UK company
www.hachette.co.uk
www.hachettechildrens.co.uk

Produced for Wayland by
White-Thomson Publishing Ltd
www.wtpub.co.uk
+44 (0)843 208 7460

The History Detective Investigates series:
Ancient Egypt
Ancient Greece
Ancient Sumer
Anglo-Saxons
Benin 900-1897 CE
Castles
The Celts
The Civil Wars
Early Islamic Civilization
The Indus Valley
The Industrial Revolution
Local History
Mayan Civilization
Monarchs
The Normans and the Battle of Hastings
Post-War Britain
The Shang Dynasty of Ancient China
Stone Age to Iron Age
Tudor Exploration
Tudor Home
Tudor Medicine
Tudor Theatre
Tudor War
Victorian Crime
Victorian Factory
Victorian School
Victorian Transport
The Vikings
Weapons and Armour Through the Ages
Monarchs
Women in World War II
Evacuation in World War II
Air Raids in World War II
Rationing in World War II

CONTENTS

Evacuation 4

Evacuation Orders 6

Getting Ready 8

Departure 10

Pictures and Propaganda 12

Finding Billets 14

Host Families 16

School Logbooks 18

Medical Reports 20

Different Voices 22

Entertainment 24

Going Home 26

Your Project 28

Glossary 30

Puzzle Answers 31

Index 32

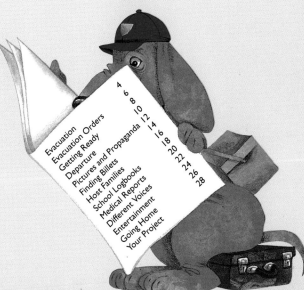

EVACUATION

Why were thousands of British children evacuated from their homes in 1939? Where did these evacuees go? How did they feel? It is still possible to find out. There are many clues, if only we know where to look. By finding them, we can follow a trail into the past which leads us to the biggest evacuation ever to take place in Britain.

When the Second World War began in 1939, people were afraid that thousands of civilians would be killed by German aeroplanes dropping bombs on British cities. So, the British Government organized an evacuation. They moved civilians away from cities to 'reception areas' in the countryside, which would not be bombed.

Most evacuees were children between the ages of 5 and 14, and mothers with young children under 5.

These children were evacuated from London. The colour pictures on page 5 give us clues about what the evacuees took with them.

Evacuees were issued with an identification label like this one. On it was written their name and the school they had come from.

LONDON COUNTY COUNCIL

Platt Edith

STARCROSS SCHOOL
ST PANCRAS N.W.1
P.T.O.

For those of us born after 1945, it is difficult to understand what evacuation must have felt like. When children were first evacuated, they had no idea how long the war would last, or when they would see their families again. Can you imagine being separated from your family for as long as six years?

Evacuees left behind many clues, which can tell us about their experiences. Government reports, newspapers, letters, photographs and school logbooks can all reveal information about the evacuation. The cartoon detective Sherlock Bones will show you where to find this evidence.

Evacuees carried gas masks like this one in case German aeroplanes dropped bombs containing poisonous gas.

NO NEED TO WONDER SEE PAGE SEVEN

Evening Despatch 6·30

PIANOS of QUALITY EXCHANGES EASY PAYMENTS SCOTCHERS CORPORATION STREET OPEN ALL DAY SATURDAYS

No. 15,026. Weather: Fair, Warm   THURSDAY, 31 AUGUST, 1939.   Radio: Page 3   ONE PENNY.

EVACUATION OF SCHOOLCHILDREN TO BEGIN TO-MORROW — *Official*

SUDDEN DECISION IS "ONLY A PRECAUTION"

Birmingham And Smethwick Affected

EVACUATION OF SCHOOLCHILDREN AND OTHER PRIORITY CLASSES FROM ALL TOWNS INCLUDED IN THE GOVERNMENT'S EVACUATION SCHEME

General view of the fire damage at the Regis Brickworks at Blackheath early to-day. Many men were thrown temporarily out of work, and the origin of the fire is a mystery. See story on Page Seven.

HITLER'S REPLY EXPECTED SOON

BRITAIN'S DEFENCE MINISTERS DISCUSS

SOVIET DISCUSSING GERMAN PACT
A JOINT session of the Supreme Soviet has been summoned for 7.30 p.m. (3.30 p.m. British summer time) to-day to discuss the ratification of the German-Soviet non-aggression pact.

DIARY OF TO-DAY'S EVENTS
9.45: Premier takes a 10-minute walk.
9.30: South African High Commissioner at the Dominions Office.
10.5: Lord and Lady Halifax and Sir

WOMAN SAID TO HAVE HAD 4 REVOLVERS

TOLD LANDLADY SHE WAS WRITING SHORT STORIES
—*Prosecution*

SMILING broadly in the dock, a slim, fair woman, who was sent for trial on an explosives charge at Cardiff today, was said to have explained her week-end trips to London to her landlady by saying she was visiting her sister who was a patient in Guy's Hospital.
She was Barbara Jones, aged 22, of no fixed abode, who was charged with having in her possession four revolvers, 79 rounds of revolver ammunition and 83 sticks of gelignite. In such circumstances as to give rise to a

This newspaper was published on 31 August 1939.

SHERLOCK BONES

Wherever you see one of Sherlock's paw-prints, like this, you will find a mystery to solve. The answers can all be found on page 31 and there are clues in the book.

🐾 What is the girl in the centre of the photograph on page 4 carrying in the square cardboard box?

🐾 Why do the children in the photograph on page 4 wear labels?

🐾 How many of the newspaper headlines are about the war?

🐾 Some evacuees were not human! Can you think what they might have been? (There is a big clue on page 29.)

EVACUATION ORDERS

EVACUATION FROM LONDON

OFFICIAL PARTIES

Evacuation is available for
SCHOOL CHILDREN
MOTHERS with CHILDREN
living in the London evacuation area

ASSISTED PRIVATE EVACUATION

A free travel voucher and billeting allowance will be given to
MOTHERS with CHILDREN
AGED and BLIND PEOPLE
INFIRM and INVALIDS
living in evacuation area who have made
arrangements with relatives or friends
for accommodation in a safer area

★ *For information ask at the Council Offices*

The Government's evacuation scheme had been planned by the 'Anderson Committee', a group led by Sir John Anderson. We can find clues about what they discussed and the decisions they made by looking at their report.

The Anderson Committee met between May and July 1938. They called in experts from railway companies, teachers and the police to advise them. To track down the Anderson Committee Report, you will have to visit the Public Record Office at Kew in London. You can find the address at the back of this book. All of the Government documents concerning the war can be seen at the Public Record Office.

If you get a chance to visit the Public Record Office in Kew, ask the archivist to help you find the Anderson Committee Report. The main recommendations of the Report are shown below.

Posters like the one on the left were put up in areas where evacuation was going to take place.

The Anderson Committee Recommendations

- Factories have to be kept open to produce important materials. People who are not doing essential jobs should be moved away from these factories, which will be targets for bombing.

- Evacuation should not be compulsory.

- Children not being evacuated with their mothers will be taken in school parties, with their teachers.

- Evacuees will be housed in private dwellings. People in the reception areas will have to look after evacuees if they are asked to do so.

🐾 If you had been in charge of evacuation plans, would you have made it compulsory for all people not doing essential work to go? See what Sherlock thinks on page 31.

Women at work in 1940, in a factory making artillery shells.

❧ Why do you think these women were not evacuated?

The children below are getting ready to be evacuated.

❧ Why do you think these evacuees are trying on new boots?

DETECTIVE WORK

Go to your local reference library, and ask to see microfilm of the local newspapers for 1938. Using a microfilm viewer, look through the headlines. Try to find the earliest mention of evacuation plans, and any reference to the Anderson Committee.

TO PARENTS
IMPORTANT NOTICE
The Government wishes it to be known that all school children living in this evacuation area should now be sent to safer districts
REGISTER AT ONCE AT

GETTING READY

The British evacuation was called 'Operation Pied Piper'. It began on Friday 1 September 1939. The Government sent parents a list, telling them what they needed to pack for their children. Some parents could not afford all the items on the list.

The children in the photograph below were evacuated as early as 1938, because people thought that the war was about to start. Their teddy bears offered some comfort. Children evacuated later in the main evacuation of 1939 were often not allowed to bring toys or teddies. Some smuggled them along in their gas mask cases.

An evacuee's teddy bear.

Evacuees clutching their teddy bears.

GOVERNMENT EVACUATION SCHEME
TO PARENTS OF SCHOOL CHILDREN

The Government have decided that parents of schoolchildren in this area are to have the opportunity of sending their children away to a safer district while present enemy activity continues. If you wish your child to go with the organised scheme, please fill in the form attached to this notice and get your child to bring it to school.

Arrangements to be made.

1. **Clothing.** Your child should take the following in addition to what he or she is wearing, and all articles must be darned and mended. If any of these articles cannot be provided please notify the teacher at once.

BOY.	GIRL.
2 vests.	2 vests.
2 under pants.	2 liberty bodices (if worn).
2 shirts.	2 knickers.
2 pyjamas or night shirts.	2 nightdresses or pyjamas.
2 pairs socks.	2 pairs socks or stockings.
2 pairs boots or shoes.	2 pairs shoes.
1 Wellingtons (if possible).	1 Wellingtons (if possible).
1 warm coat and/or mackintosh. (if not being worn).	1 warm coat and/or mackintosh.
1 pair knickers or trousers.	1 warm dress or tunic and jersey.
1 pullover.	1 cardigan.
6 handkerchiefs.	2 cotton frocks.
1 toothbrush.	6 handkerchiefs.
1 face flannel.	1 toothbrush
1 comb	1 face flannel.
2 towels	1 comb
	2 towels

Gas mask
Identity card
Ration book
Clothing and personal coupons

2. You will wish to do everything possible to ensure that your child goes away with clean clothes, clean hair and a clean body

3. **Luggage.** The child should wear his warmest and thickest footwear. The inventory above is to be taken as minimum requirements, but do remember that your child should not take more than he can carry comfortably.

4. **Food.** Each child should take sufficient food for one day. Be sure your child has his ration book and if pages of coupons out of his book have been deposited with retailers, ask for their return and pin the loose pages in the ration book. Your child's ration book, identity card and personal coupons should be packed inside the gas mask case.

PLEASE keep this notice for reference and return the form to your child's school **immediately** if you want him or her to take part in the evacuation scheme.

———————— cut here ————————

The document above was sent out to parents to tell them what evacuees should take with them.

🐾 **What does this document tell us children kept in their gas mask case?**

Try to find out whether you are living in an area which was evacuated, or in a 'reception area' to which evacuees travelled. You could interview relatives who lived through the war. If you live in an evacuated area, you could ask them what they took with them on their journey.

An evacuee's rucksack.

🐾 Where was the evacuee who owned the rucksack above going to stay?

Children waiting with their rucksacks to be evacuated from Gravesend in Essex.

🐾 Look up Gravesend on a map. What form of transport do you think might have been used to carry parties of evacuees away from here?

DETECTIVE WORK

Many important clues can be found in your local Record Office. This is usually found in the main town in your area, where the County Council has its offices. To use the Record Office, phone up and book a table. Tell the archivist which documents you would like to see.

When you arrive at the Record Office, you can use the catalogue to find documents, or ask the archivist for help. When you find a document you wish to see, copy its reference number on to a form at the archivist's desk. The archivist will then find you the document.

DEPARTURE

Most evacuees travelled to city railway stations to begin their journey to the countryside. Special timetables had to be arranged for the many extra train services. The evacuees did not even know where they were travelling to.

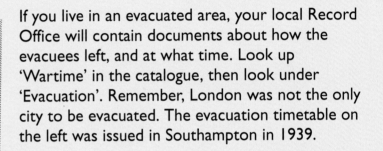

EVACUATION TIMETABLE

If you live in an evacuated area, your local Record Office will contain documents about how the evacuees left, and at what time. Look up 'Wartime' in the catalogue, then look under 'Evacuation'. Remember, London was not the only city to be evacuated. The evacuation timetable on the left was issued in Southampton in 1939.

❧ Look carefully at the document. What sort of people were evacuated?

❧ At what date and time did the evacuation start from Bitterne Park Infants?

Timetables like the one above were posted on school gates and noticeboards in areas which were being evacuated.

This photograph shows the timetable changes at London's Charing Cross Station caused by the evacuation of children.

If you live in a reception area, you should be able to find documents which tell you at what time evacuees were arriving, and where they were coming from. The document below was found by looking up 'Wartime', then looking under 'Air Raid Precautions' in the Dorchester Record Office.

Air Raid Precautions
Disposition of secondary school children from Croydon

Railhead	Dorsetshire Secondary School	Croydon School	Estimated number of Croydon children
Poole	Poole Grammar (Boys)	Tennison	150
Swanage	Swanage Grammar (Mixed)	Ruskin	350
Dorchester	Dorchester High School (Girls)	Girls' High School	750

30 SEPTEMBER 1938

DETECTIVE WORK

Some trains carrying evacuees stopped at small village stations called 'halts'. Many of these were closed down in the 1960s. If there was a station in your area, try to find out if it was used for evacuees. You may be able to find a book about your local railway which contains a map. Use this map to locate the station, and try to find out what has happened to it today.

🐾 What does the document above tell us about evacuees attending Swanage Grammar School?

Evacuees get ready to board their train.

🐾 How do we know that the children in this picture were being evacuated from Croydon?

Pictures and Propaganda

Many of our ideas about how evacuees felt come from photographs taken at the time. We are often shown images of children with smiling faces going off on an adventure. There is hardly a tear in sight. But is this how evacuees really felt?

As history detectives, we need to think carefully about why a photograph was taken. Some photographs were taken for 'propaganda'. This means that the photographer wanted people to believe in a particular point of view.

For example, the Government published photographs which showed evacuees looking extremely happy. They did this so that evacuees would not be afraid of evacuation, and so that parents would not worry as much about their missing children. For a history detective, photographs like this may contain false clues.

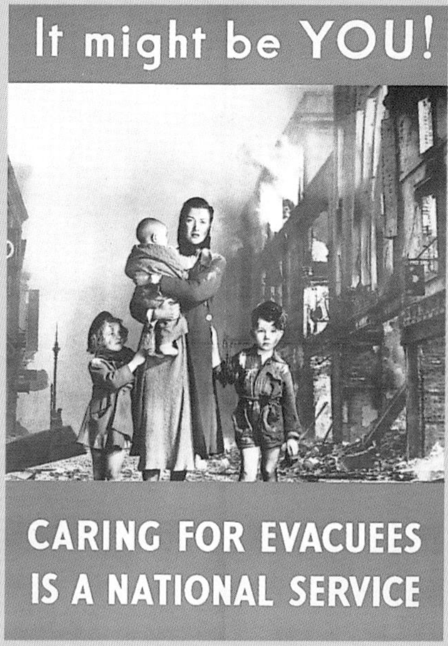
It might be YOU!
CARING FOR EVACUEES
IS A NATIONAL SERVICE

This poster was printed by the Ministry of Health.

Why do you think the poster above was printed?

The evacuees below look extremely cheerful. The woman on the platform does not look quite so happy!

THIRD

To give you an impression of how a photograph can be used for propaganda, look carefully at the picture on the right. Write down some words describing the children. Where might they be going? Can we tell that they are leaving home to live with strangers?

THIRD

Now look at a different part of the same photograph, shown on the left. How do you think the little boy feels? Where do you think he might be going? This evacuee gives us a very different impression. He is leaving home to live with strangers and he does not know when he will see his parents again.

🐾 Why do you think this boy was often cut out of the picture? Does your reason match Sherlock's on page 31?

This is a good lesson to learn. When you come across any photographic evidence in your search, you need to ask questions about the clues it contains.

DETECTIVE WORK

Try to track down a photograph of evacuees. You may find an old postcard or book in a second-hand shop. Ask yourself three questions. Who took the picture? Why did they take it? Might the picture have been taken for propaganda?

FINDING BILLETS

Remember that the Anderson Committee said evacuees should live with people in private houses. These houses were called 'billets'. A local 'billeting officer' was appointed to find suitable houses in all the areas which were receiving evacuees.

In January and February 1939 the Government conducted an 'accommodation census' to find out how many billets were available. Local people called 'visitors' interviewed householders in reception areas, and filled in census forms. Officials used these forms to decide how many evacuees could be billeted in each area.

In the Record Office you may find a Summary of Accommodation, like the one below. This one reveals the total number of billets in Hove, Sussex, and shows how many extra blankets and mattresses were needed for evacuees.

The pub above was converted into a billeting office which found homes for evacuees.

This Summary of Accommodation enabled the Ministry of Health to plan for an evacuation to Hove.

GOVERNMENT EVACUATION SCHEME.
Form Ev. 4
Encl. to Cir. 1789.

MINISTRY OF HEALTH.
Summary of Accommodation.

County SUSSEX – EAST
County Borough, Borough,
Urban or Rural District OF HOVE

(In rural districts a separate return is required for each parish and a summary for the district as a whole.)

	Total number of habitable rooms.	Total Number of additional persons who could be accommodated.	Provisional decision of Local Authority as to numbers to be accommodated.					Additional bedding required.			
			Unaccompanied Children.	Teachers and Helpers.	Others.	Accommodation reserved privately.	Total.	Mattresses.		Blankets.	
								Double.	Single.	Double.	Single.
Private Houses	84,216.	21,796.	6,282.	1,019	374 c / 560 d / 6180 e	3,256.	17,671.	475.	1,271.	927.	2,864.
Hotels and boarding houses H.	1,020.	125.	17.	13.	57 e						
BH.	1,448.	359.	51.	10.	2 c / 4 d / 174 e	4.	332.				
Empty houses	5,820.	5 820 (Ins)									
Camps, Hostels, etc.	NiL						✓				
TOTALS	92,504.	28,100 (Ins) / 22,280.	6,350.	1,042.	7351.	3,260.	18,003.	475.	1,271.	927.	2,864.

(A) INCLUDING SELF-CONTAINED FLATS.
(B) EXCLUDING PUBLIC HOUSES.
(C) MOTHERS WITH (D) CHILDREN.
(E) OTHERS – ADULTS, MALE & FEMALE.

H) HOTELS.
BOARDING HOUSES.

(3668) Wt. 37036/9333 30m 1/39 S.E.R. Ltd. Gp. 662

Signed_____ Wernyn Hamson
Town Clerk to the Local Authority. R HOVE
Date _____ 8th March 1939.

❧ Examine the Summary of Accommodation for Hove. How many teachers and helpers could stay in hotels and boarding houses?

❧ What would happen if 30,000 evacuees arrived in Hove?

EMERGENCY HOUSING

SPARE ROOMS
URGENTLY NEEDED

The Government is asking householders to let their spare rooms, furnished or unfurnished. Many men and women coming back from the Services want temporary homes. *In this district the need is urgent.*

WILL **YOU** HELP?

If you have a spare room, or rooms, you can let, you should fix the rent and register the letting with the Local Council. Then your right to get the rooms back when you need them will be protected under the law; and any clause in your tenancy or lease forbidding sub-letting will be waived.

FOR FURTHER INFORMATION
APPLY TO:

The Government published posters asking for extra accommodation.

In spite of all the planning, some serious mistakes were made. In Berkshire, for example, billets were found for 23,915 evacuees but 46,722 evacuees arrived. The billeting officers had to go from house to house asking people to take extra evacuees. This upset hosts who suddenly had to make more room. It also left many evacuees feeling unwanted.

Some evacuees arrived in the countryside to find that there were not enough billets.

DETECTIVE WORK

At your local reference library, look through the microfilm of your local newspapers from 1939. Look out for clues in the headlines. Make a note of any stories which deal with evacuees being billeted. The headline below comes from the *Dorset County Chronicle and Swanage Times* on 7 September 1939.

NEARLY 4,000 EVACUEES IN DORCHESTER. FOUR DAYS BILLETING.

HOST FAMILIES

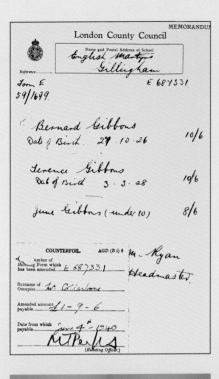

After a journey which was often long and tiring, evacuees had to line up and wait for a 'host family' to choose them. Waiting to be chosen was often the worst part of their ordeal. Can you imagine how it felt if you were one of the last to be picked?

Hosts received money for each evacuee they took in. They were paid by taking a form to the local post office. Your Record Office may still have forms or receipts showing that hosts had been paid.

The payment slip on the left shows that a family in Gillingham in June 1940 received 10 shillings and 6 pence (10/6) a week for each child over 10, and 8 shillings and 6 pence for younger children. To give you an idea of what this was worth, a farm labourer earned about 38 shillings a week.

A host's payment slip.

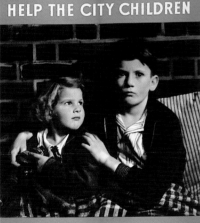

A Government poster, urging people to provide billets.

Evacuees meeting their host family. The man on the left is probably the billeting officer.

❀ If the evacuees in the photograph above arrived in Gillingham in 1940 and were aged 5, 8, 11 and 12, how much would their hosts have been paid each week? (There were 12 pence in a shilling.)

DETECTIVE WORK

Visit the Record Office, and look up the files labelled 'Correspondence' for 1939. From the clues in these letters, write an account of how different hosts felt about looking after evacuees.

Billeting was compulsory. People who refused to take evacuees into their homes without a good reason could be taken to court and fined. The fine was usually 15 shillings, but in August 1940 a man in Dorset was fined £5 for refusing to house two children.

You may find letters in the Record Office which show people describing their reasons for not taking evacuees. These letters can be found in files labelled 'Correspondence'. The letter on the right comes from the Devon Record Office, in Exeter.

1.12.40
From Doctor.
With reference to Lady Davy: On medical grounds it is not good for her to have ten evacuees in a house with only 5 bedrooms and 2 living rooms. Because of her public duties, Lady Davy requires more than just her bedroom.

This woman in Chichester offered many evacuees a home.

SCHOOL LOGBOOKS

It was not only billets that had to be found for evacuees. They also needed schools. Many teachers had been evacuated with their pupils, but it was not always easy to find them classrooms to teach in.

These evacuees from London used an open-air classroom.

❀ The teacher in this photograph is quite elderly. Why do you think she was still teaching?

In school logbooks for 1939–45, head teachers wrote down the problems faced by their school during the war. You can track down these logbooks in the local Record Office, where they are listed in the catalogue under 'Education'. The following extract is taken from the logbook for Bradfield Village School in Berkshire.

> ## Oct. 4th 1939.
> On instructions from the LEA the children evacuated by the LCC were admitted to school this morning. 57 children were admitted bringing the number on roll up to 206. There is insufficient seating for all the children and some are sitting 3 to a dual desk.

❀ What do LEA and LCC stand for? You can find the answer somewhere in this book.

In the following year, Bradfield School admitted 184 new children, most of them evacuees. By finding more clues in the logbook, we can discover that the school received help with the desks.

> ## Nov. 1st 1939.
> Received from the LCC, 25 tables and 50 chairs for the use of the evacuees.

DETECTIVE WORK

Many city schools were left empty after the evacuation. Some were used for first aid posts and as decontamination centres. Try to find out what happened to your town's schools during the war. Were they evacuated and used for some other purpose? Or were they used for evacuees?

In some places it was impossible to teach all the children in one building. Other arrangements had to be made, as a logbook from a school in Reading shows.

Feb. 26th 1940.

... classes in the Junior department are still receiving instruction in the afternoon sessions at Park Institute, Anderson Baptist Chapel and the Primitive Methodist Chapel.

The boys in the photograph below are being evacuated from their school in Addlestone, Surrey, in 1941.

Why do you think these schoolboys were evacuated? Sherlock has found a clue.

MEDICAL REPORTS

You may read stories of evacuees being dirty, having head lice and spreading infections such as ringworm and impetigo. But if you look at school medical reports from before the war, you will see that it was not only evacuees who had these health problems.

Evacuees arriving in South Wales after their journey from the Midlands.

🐾 Examine the photograph carefully. Can you find people from two different organizations who helped evacuees when they arrived?

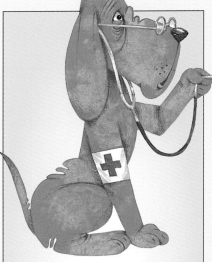

DETECTIVE WORK

Visit your local Record Office, and try to find the County Council Minutes for 1938 in your area. Look for reports written by the School Medical Officer. These may show that there were major outbreaks of illness at local schools long before the evacuation began.

In his annual report of 1938, the School Medical Officer in Dorset made the following report.

> **Medical Report, Dorset, 1938**
> Total number of children in the county excluded from school because of medical conditions: 255 impetigo, 70 ringworm, 13 scabies and 98 in a verminous condition.

🐾 What do the date and location of the Medical Officer's report tell us?

🐾 Rumours about 'dirty evacuees' started almost as soon as they arrived in some reception areas. Why do you think some evacuees looked untidy after their journey?

During the first evacuation in 1939, it was impossible for all evacuees to be medically examined, so some children did arrive with illnesses. However, during a second evacuation in 1940, doctors were able to examine more evacuees before they left home.

Young evacuees receive a health check before they depart.

Remember that not all evacuees came from poor areas. Some children found themselves evacuated from homes with bathrooms, to billets which had no facilities except a toilet at the bottom of the garden and a tin bath in front of the fire.

In 1944, a Women's Institute survey found that in 21 counties 50 per cent of village schools had only earth or bucket toilets. In one school in Wantage, children had to have breaks at different times because there were not enough toilets.

These evacuees left London quite late in the war, in 1942. The boy is very smartly dressed.

DIFFERENT VOICES

By reading their accounts and letters, we can see that the experiences of evacuees varied greatly. The following account comes from a child evacuated from Liverpool to Wales.

Evacuees at a miner's house in Wales.

We were chosen by a lady and taken to her house. We were sent around to the back door and told to strip off all our clothing. When we refused, our clothes were torn off. We were then forced naked into the kitchen in front of the host's father and husband and pushed into a tin bath containing Dettol. After this her husband cut all our hair off until we were bald. His excuse was that children from Liverpool brought lice, scabies and sores into the countryside. When we were taken to school the next day we met other children evacuated to the area and they were also totally bald.

Lillian Evans, in *Yesterday's Children*

The account and photograph above are both clues telling us about evacuees in Wales, but they show two very different pictures of evacuation.

This newspaper was published on 2 September 1939.

Letters and newspaper reports can both give us clues about how refugees felt. Some evacuees were extremely happy with their hosts, as the letter below, from a girl evacuated to Cornwall, shows.

HILDE MARCHANT brings mothers a message of comfort from the country

FLORENCE, FROM HOLBORN, E.C., SEES HER FIRST VILLAGE

Palace guard wear war kit

Beginning of a new life

'Why, the houses have straw hats'

By HILDE MARCHANT

Mrs S. was with the WVS and still had a petrol ration and took me out in her car. I was happy and took their dog 'Rufus' for long walks which he needed as he was too fat for a spaniel.

🐾 In the newspaper, Florence talks of 'houses with straw hats'. What does she mean by this, and what does this tell us about her?

DETECTIVE WORK

Try to find someone in your area who was an evacuee or lived in a reception area. Ask if you can interview them. If possible, get their permission to record the interview on tape. Sherlock has some questions you could ask.

TO AN EX-EVACUEE:

Where were you evacuated from?

What did you take with you?

Can you describe your journey?

Can you describe your hosts and billet?

TO SOMEONE WHO LIVED IN A RECEPTION AREA:

Did you have evacuees living in your house?

How did you feel about the evacuees?

Where did the evacuees come from?

Did the evacuees stay very long?

Evacuees from London arriving in Cornwall.

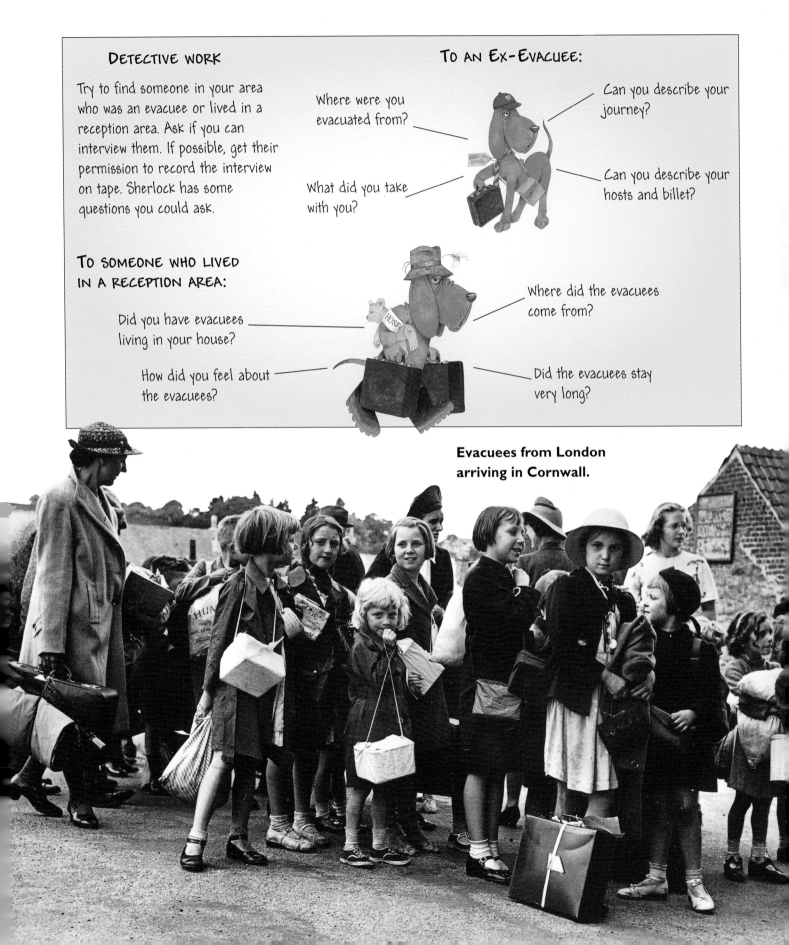

ENTERTAINMENT

ecause there were no bombing raids at the beginning of the war, many evacuees returned home. The Government was afraid that if they did not stop evacuees going back to the cities, they would be killed by later bombing. In December 1939, the Government introduced entertainments to make the evacuees want to stay where they were.

CHILDREN
are safer in the country
. . . leave them there

The Government poster above urged parents to let evacuated children remain in the countryside.

Evacuees from London at a Christmas party in Shenfield, Essex.

There were no special trains organized to take children home for Christmas, in case they decided to stay for good. Instead, Christmas parties and pantomimes were organized in reception areas. The parties were so successful that they were repeated in some areas every Christmas until 1944.

DETECTIVE WORK

At your local library, search through microfilm showing copies of your local paper from December to January between 1939 and 1944. You should find evidence of parties and entertainments in your area. Copy the headlines and reports, and use them to make your own wartime newspaper.

DORSET COUNTY CHRONICLE
7 Dec 1939
Christmas parties for evacuees to be arranged in villages

Evacuees from Greenwich, below, wave goodbye to the Mayor of Greenwich after his visit.

Sometimes, parties were attended by the mayor of the area where the evacuees came from. This provided evacuees with a link to their home. Evacuees also put on shows for their hosts. These shows were reported in local newspapers like those shown in Sherlock's hands and below. They can give you another view of the evacuees' experiences.

RETFORD TIMES, 15 December 1939

TOWN HALL CROWDED FOR CONCERT

Since they became Retford's guests the evacuee children from Leeds have won a well-deserved reputation in the staging of public entertainment. The Town Hall was packed on Thursday for another of their concerts during which the senior boys sang a special song.

GOING HOME

In April 1945, the Government sent out a timetable of travel arrangements to return the evacuees to their homes when the war was over. The return of the evacuees was much better organized than the original evacuation in 1939 had been.

Returning evacuees to their homes was not as easy as you might think. Some evacuees returned to find their homes destroyed by bombs. Others, whose parents had been killed, had nobody to go home to. Some evacuees could not even be found, because they had gone home early without telling anyone!

This homeless evacuee had to be housed in the hostels you can see behind him.

The Government made the plans listed in the box below, for those children returning to London.

Arrangements for Return

- The County Councils appointed someone to get the evacuees to the correct station.
- The London County Council appointed a Train Marshal who had to arrange overnight stays, and looked after all the luggage. He was helped by volunteers who travelled with the children.
- A Feeding Executive Officer was placed in charge of feeding the evacuees. All evacuees were given a packed lunch for the train, and received a meal when they arrived in London.
- All luggage was given special coloured labels, that showed which centre evacuees had to go to when they arrived in London.

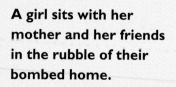

A girl sits with her mother and her friends in the rubble of their bombed home.

You can see the joy in these evacuees' faces as they are reunited with their parents.

DETECTIVE WORK

By searching the microfilm at your local library, you should be able to find a number of local newspaper reports about evacuees returning home.

Copy the headlines and reports, and add them to your own wartime newspaper.

By 12 July 1945, 54,317 evacuees had returned to London. Over one hundred trains were used to transport them.

By August 1945 there were still 76,000 people in reception areas. These were people who either had no home to go to, or who did not want to return. When evacuation officially finished in March 1946, there were still 5,200 evacuees remaining in the reception areas. In one way or another, evacuees would be affected by their experiences for the rest of their lives.

YOUR PROJECT

You should now be able to find all the clues you need to solve the mystery of the British evacuation. But you must decide on a topic to investigate. Choose one which interests you and is suitable for the area you live in. You may wish to use one of the following questions as your title.

After your investigation, you should be able to say what is written on these evacuees' labels, what is in their suitcases and why they are wearing wellington boots.

Topic Questions
- How did evacuees travel?
- Who planned the evacuation?
- What did a billeting officer do?
- How did evacuation affect my school?
- What entertainments were organized for evacuees?
- Who organized the return home?

You must also decide how you want to present your project. You could include the following ideas.

Project Presentation
- Illustrate your project with diagrams, photographs and drawings.
- Make a wall chart of the pictures and documents you have used.
- Present your project in the form of an evacuee's diary.
- Use interviews recorded on a tape recorder or video.
- Copy newspaper reports and make them into your own Second World War newspaper.

If you are a determined history detective you may even find out something unusual about evacuation. For example, Sherlock discovered from the newspaper report and photograph below that some people even evacuated their pets.

Dorset County Chronicle and Swanage Times, 2 Nov 1939

The Animal Defence Society ... organized a smoothly working animal evacuation scheme. Already hundreds of cats and dogs have been sent out of London to carefully chosen homes in the country and more are leaving every day. The Duchess of Hamilton, who is president of the society, stated: 'If any of your readers would like an animal for the time being, I can promise them plenty to choose from, and they will know that they are making some poor person very happy and really doing something to help their country.'

Evacuees and a pet dog in their schoolroom.

GLOSSARY

archivist Someone who looks after the documents at a Record Office.

billets The houses and hostels where evacuees stayed.

catalogue A list of items, usually written in alphabetical order.

civilians People who are not in the armed forces.

compulsory Required by law.

contribution Something given, such as a payment.

correspondence Letters.

decontamination centre A place where the effects of poison gas are cleaned up.

evacuation The movement of people from areas of danger to areas where they will be safe.

impetigo A skin disease which is passed on easily from one person to another.

LCC Abbreviation for London County Council.

LEA Abbreviation for Local Education Authority.

microfilm A film on which you can find whole newspapers or written documents reduced to a small size.

propaganda Written information, film, photographs or posters, which are used to put over a certain message or point of view.

reception areas Areas of the country, thought to be safe, to which evacuees were sent.

ringworm A skin disease, usually found on the head, which can leave circular bare patches.

scabies A skin disease causing severe itching, which is easily passed from one person to another.

verminous Infested with insects, such as lice.

WVS Abbreviation for the Women's Voluntary Service, an organization of women volunteers who provided important wartime services, such as escorting evacuees on their journeys.

BOOKS TO READ
Non-fiction
My War: Evacuee by Peter Hepplewhite (Wayland, 2005)
At Home in World War II: Evacuation by Stewart Ross (Evans Brothers, 2001)
History Journeys: An Evacuee's Journey by Peter Hepplewhite (Wayland, 2004)

Fiction
Carrie's War by Nina Bawden (Penguin, 2003) An adventure story about children who have been evacuated to Wales.
Goodnight Mr Tom by Michelle Magorian (Longman, 2000) The story of the relationship between an evacuee and his elderly host.

Children can use this book to improve their literacy skills in the following ways:

- ✓ To identify different types of text, and to understand the use of fact and opinion (Year 4, Term 1, Non-fiction reading comprehension).

- ✓ To identify the different purposes of evacuation timetables, plans and instructions (Year 3, Term 2, Non-fiction reading comprehension).

- ✓ To identify newspaper features, predict newspaper stories from headlines, and to write newspaper-style reports (Year 4, Term 1, Non-fiction reading comprehension and writing composition).

- ✓ To evaluate Government advertisements for their impact, appeal and honesty (Year 4, Term 3, Non-fiction reading comprehension).

PUZZLE ANSWERS

Page 5

- The girl is carrying her gas mask in the box.
- Some evacuees became separated from their school parties during the confusion at railway stations, so these labels allowed them to be identified.
- Three: 'Evacuation of Schoolchildren', 'Britain's Defence Ministers' and 'Soviet Discussing German Pact'.
- Some people's pets were evacuated.

Page 6

- It would have been very difficult to make evacuation compulsory. Some people wished to stay in their own homes. Others wished to look after their businesses or stay with relatives. It would also have been difficult to find enough billets if everyone had been evacuated.

Page 7

- They were not evacuated because their work, packing artillery shells, was vital for supplying the armed forces.
- The evacuees needed new boots because they were being evacuated from city streets to the muddy lanes of the countryside.

Page 8

- Children were instructed to keep their ration book, identity card and personal coupons inside their gas mask case.

Page 9

- The owner of the rucksack was going to stay in Talbot Road, Bromley, Kent. (It is written on the rucksack.)
- Children were evacuated from Gravesend down the Thames, on ships and boats.

Page 10

- The evacuees were schoolchildren, teachers and registered helpers, children under five with mother or other adult, expectant mothers, the blind, and people who were lame but were not in wheelchairs.
- The evacuation started from Bitterne Park Infants on Friday 1 September, not later than 6.30 am.

Page11

- Both boys and girls attended Swanage Grammar, because it was a 'mixed' school. Evacuees from Ruskin School in Croydon were sent there.
- Croydon is written in chalk on the platform.

Page 12

- The poster was meant to shock people into offering their homes to evacuees. The image of the bombed family would make people feel sorry for those suffering the destruction of air raids.

Page 13

- The photograph would have been cut because the Government wanted to persuade people that evacuees were safe and enjoying a great adventure. If they showed the little boy, he would make parents worry that their own children were homesick.

Page 14

- Thirteen teachers could stay in Hove hotels, and ten in boarding houses.
- An extra 28,100 people could be housed in Hove. If 30,000 arrived, billeting officers would have to knock on doors and advertise in newspapers to find extra rooms. You can see from the handwritten correction that a decision has already been made to use 5,820 rooms in empty houses.

Page 16

- The host family would have received 21 shillings for the two evacuees over 10 (10 shillings, six pence x 2) and 17 shillings for the two evacuees under 10 (8 shillings, 6 pence x 2). This gives a total of 38 shillings, the same as a farm labourer's wages.

Page 18

- Many teachers had been called up to serve in the armed forces, so some retired teachers were asked to take over classes.
- The glossary tells you that LEA stands for the Local Education Authority, LCC for the London County Council.

Page 19

- They were evacuated because their school had burnt down. You can see the ruins in the background.

Page 20

- People from the Girl Guides and St John's Ambulance are shown in the photograph helping the arriving evacuees.
- The report was written before the war in a reception area. This tells us that illnesses which people said were spread to the area by evacuees in 1939 were already there.
- Some children had been on trains with no toilets for up to 12 hours and had wet themselves. Others had been sick. No wonder they looked untidy.

Page 22

- Houses with straw hats were thatched cottages. Florence had clearly never been to the country and seen one before.

INDEX

Numbers in **bold** refer to pictures and captions.

accommodation census 14
Anderson Committee 6, 7, 14

billets 14, **14**, 15, **16**, 17, 18, 21, 23, 28
bombing 4, 6, 24, 26, **26**

Christmas 24, **24**
civilians 4
clothing **7**, **8**, **21**, **28**

entertainment 24, **24**, 25, **25**

factories 6, **7**
food 26

gas masks **5**, 8
Germany 4, 5
Government 4, 8, 12, 14, **15**, **16**, 24, **24**, 26

health 17, 20, 21, **21**, 22
hosts 15, 16, **16**, 23

interviews 9, 23, 28

labels 5, **5**, 26, **28**
letters 5, 17, 22
libraries 7, 15, 25, 27
logbooks 5, 18, **18**, 19, **19**
London **4**, 10, **10**, **18**, **21**, **23**, **24**, 26, 29

mayors 25, **25**

newspapers 5, **5**, 7, 15, 22, **22**, 25, 27, 28, 29

Operation Pied Piper 8

parents 4, 6, 8, 26, **27**
payment 16, **16**
pets 22, 29, **29**
photographs 5, 12, 13, **13**, 22, 29
posters **6**, **12**, **15**, **16**, 24
propaganda 12, 13, **13**

railways 6, 10, 11, **13**, 20
reception areas 4, 6, 9, 11, 14, 20, 23, 24, 27
Record Office 6, 9, 10, 14, 16, 17, 18, 20
reports 5, 6, 20, **20**
returning home 26, 27, **27**, 28

schools 5, 6, 10, 11, 18, 19, **19**, 20, 28, **29**
Summary of Accommodation 14

teachers 6, 14, 18, **18**
timetables 10, **10**, 26
toilets 21
toys 8, **8**
transport 6, 9, 10, 11, **13**, 20, 22, 26, 27, 28

Wales **20**, 22, **22**